welcome
Beloved

"Yes, I have loved you with an everlasting love; Therefore with lovingkindness I have drawn you." - Jeremiah 31:3

You are the beloved of God. It is who you are. No one can take that away from you, ever. You are your Heavenly Father's cherished and valued daughter; the apple of His eye. You are known, you are seen, you are adored, you are beautiful, and you are perfect in His eyes.

The Bible is His love letter to you. It chronicles His pursuit of your heart since the beginning of time. His relentless, reckless, all-consuming love for you was demonstrated through Jesus Christ's life, death & resurrection. He craved intimacy and oneness with you and that is exactly what Jesus has given you. Seek after His heart, and you will discover wonders beyond anything you could imagine. Along your journey your faith will grow stronger; strong enough to uphold you through all trials. You will be Jesus strong!

Your Bible Time Journal is your intimate interaction with your Beloved. It is His love letter to you, and yours to Him. I am so excited for you!

"As the Father loved Me, I also have loved you; abide in My love." - John 15:9

With great love, Janette

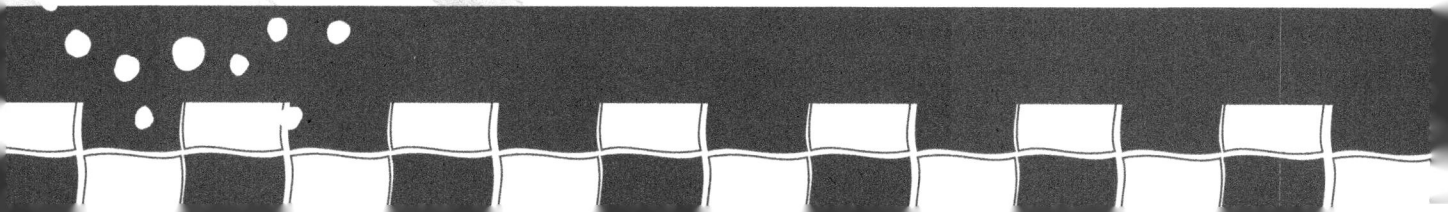

Introduction

My passion is to guide women into a personal relationship with the living God, your Creator, your Savior, Jesus Christ. To go far beyond calling yourself a Christian. To go deep into the heart of God, where you will see yourself as He sees you; His beloved child. Where you will encounter God and experience His love, His passion, His power and His guidance throughout your life. Where you will discover your purpose and value in the Kingdom of God. You were not called to be a spectator. You are called to be an influencer, an integral person, an essential ingredient in the mission of the body of Christ to this generation and even beyond. Your voice is needed. Your gifts are needed. There has never been anyone like you. The kaleidoscope of your life is unique to you. Your story, your experiences, your talents, your strengths and your weaknesses are all for a beautiful purpose in the Kingdom of God. The Bible says, *"Let no one despise your youth, but be an example to the believers in word, in conduct, in love, in spirit, in faith, in purity.* - 1Timothy 4:12. You are valued, this is your calling, and God wants to speak to you. He wants to grow you, fashion you, and empower you for your unique purpose & calling. This is living out the abundant life that Jesus promised to give you - it is yours to seize!

My daughter, Melissa Camp, lived her life to the fullest. She loved Jesus more than any person I have ever met. She discovered the secret to true happiness and fulfillment even in the midst of life's most difficult trials . She writes, "Get in the Word and you will find true happiness." She knew the Source. She was willing for all, big, or small. The journey of life was exciting as she walked every step with Jesus. He was her abundance. Her earthly life was short, a mere 21 years. It was filled with love, oh, so much love! It was filled with joy, peace, and the miraculous. Melissa is an influencer; she is an integral person, an essential ingredient in the mission of the body of Christ to this generation and beyond. Though she is dead, she is alive in Christ, and God is still using her life to impact millions for the Kingdom of God. You can read her journals and her story in the book, Melissa, If One Life . . .; you can watch the movie I STILL BELIEVE that is based on her love story with Jeremy Camp. You can listen to Jeremy's music and experience the beauty that God can bring out of suffering. Melissa's life has been my inspiration and my calling is to communicate to others that they too can live a spectacular life with eternal fruit that carries on beyond this life. Your life is meant to leave a legacy.

> *But you are a chosen generation, a royal priesthood, a holy nation, His own special people, that you may proclaim the praises of Him who called you out of darkness into His marvelous light; - 1Peter 2:9*

Bible Time journal

Dedicated

To my fun, creative, compassionate, amazing, almost teen granddaughters:
Gracie, Maci, Kenzie and Harper
and to my up and coming teen, Daphne,
and my littles, Kirra and Kili.

You are greatly loved! May you love the Lord Jesus
with all your heart all the days of your life.

Love 4ever, MeMa

BIBLE TIME JOURNAL FOR TEEN GIRLS

30 DAY PERSONAL BIBLE STUDY AND PRAYER JOURNAL FOR TEENS

Make sure to visit:

www.melissalynncamp.com

www.janettehenning.com

www.janettehenning.com/freegifts

Bible Time Journal for Teen Girls
Written and creatively compiled by Janette Henning
Copyright © 2022 Janette Henning

Your Bible Time Journal is your opportunity to discover God's voice speaking directly to you through the Word of God, the Bible. Instead of reading a devotional that someone else wrote, you will be writing your own. God wants to speak directly to your heart without the distraction of another person's voice interpreting what He is saying. We definitely need people with the gift of teaching God's Word, but do not miss out on your own time where God will show you great, and mighty things, wondrous things in His Word. You might even discover that you have the spiritual gift of teaching and communicating God's Word to others. You might discover that you are a writer and your devotions will touch the hearts of many. Use your gifts to impact others through social media. You are meant to make a difference in this world! I know God will open up new horizons for you as you encounter Him through His Word. Expect to be amazed! The following pages will explain the process of gleaning from the Word and personally experiencing Jesus through the activities. The daily accountability page will help you to maintain a connection with God throughout your day. Anticipate 30 days of wonder, amazement and transformation! You are greatly loved, my beloved.

> I pray
> that nothing takes away my hearts
> attention on You. My Father. I want to cry out
> — ABBA. Father: worthy is Your name. When I am
> down all I need is You. You brighten up my days.
> It's amazing. I know and I tell people.
> "Get in the Word and you will find true happiness."
> Abba. when I am down it is because I fail to get in the Word.
> I pray that today my spiritual goal will be that no matter
> what mood I am in I will turn to You. When I am
> sad. Father. I want to be in Your Word so that You
> can lift me up. I fail in my own strength.
> but in Your strength. I can achieve.
>
> Melissa

About
your journal

Daily accountability
Practice these activities everyday and you will walk closer to God. You will also see a transformation in your life through the renewing of your mind.

Morning prayer
Begin your morning with a short prayer releasing all your troubles into His care.

Scripture for the day
Record the Scripture or Bible passage that you are focusing on today.

Today's affirmation
Write out a positive Bible truth of your own that you can claim for your life today.

Evening praise
Visit your journal in the evening to write your praises to the Lord for all He has done for you.

3 Points of gratitude
What are 3 things that you are grateful for today? Set your mind on thankfulness and praises before you sleep.

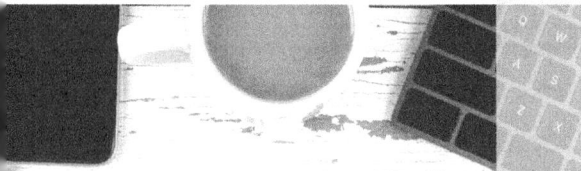

5 steps

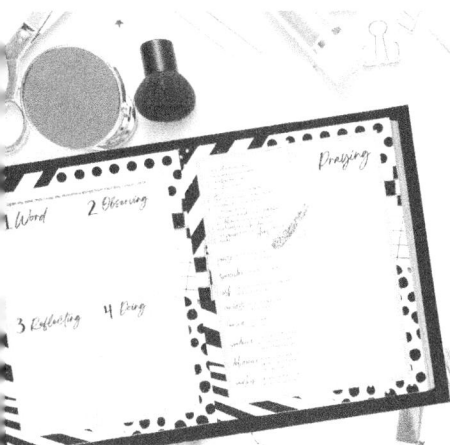

1 Word

Choose a Bible passage to read in context or start reading through a book in the Bible. Write out a verse that resonates with you.

2 Observing

Write out what you observe. Pay attention to the context, who is speaking and who they are speaking to?

3 Reflecting

What life lessons can you learn from the passage? What is God saying to you through this Scripture?

4 Doing

The book of James compels us to be doers of the Word and not hearers only. How can you apply what you have read and learned?

5 Praying & Journaling

Use the Lord's prayer as a guide to begin your prayer time. Pour out your heart to the Lord and listen for His.

Word
step one

"Open my eyes, that I may see Wondrous things from Your law." - Psalm 119:18

The Bible isn't just words on a page. It is not a story book to be read like a novel. It is supernatural, glorious, wondrous, and personal. It has the power to save lives, transform minds, heal broken hearts, and reconcile sinful men with a Holy God. It should be prized above all things, as it is the very Word of God. There are treasures in this book that can only be found with eyes opened by God to one with a believing heart.

"For the word of God is living and powerful, and sharper than any two-edged sword, piercing even to the division of soul and spirit, and of joints and marrow, and is a discerner of the thoughts and intents of the heart." - Hebrews 4:12

"All Scripture is given by inspiration of God, and is profitable for doctrine, for reproof, for correction, for instruction in righteousness, that the man of God may be complete, thoroughly equipped for every good work. - 2Timothy 3:16-17

Begin your Bible reading by asking God to open your eyes so that you may see wondrous things, that you may hear His voice piercing your heart, correcting, instructing, loving and guiding you. Make it your desire to seek Him with your whole heart, with a surrendered will, and He will reveal glorious, wondrous things, and most of all, He will reveal Himself to you.

My suggestion is to use a good study Bible, then choose a book of the Bible in the New Testament to focus on for these 30 days. One of the Gospels is a great place to start. Anticipate that the Holy Spirit will reveal something that will resonate with your heart. Keep reading until something stands out to you. It could be a specific verse or an overall thought or impression on what you have read. Write it down in the space provided.

In the beginning was the Word, and the Word was with God, and the Word was God. ... And the Word became flesh and dwelt among us, and we beheld His glory, the glory as of the only begotten of the Father, full of grace and truth. - John 1:1,14

Observing
step two

You asked the LORD to open your eyes so you could see, so what do you see? Look carefully and pay attention to the context. It is always good to read a section of Scripture so you can understand the meaning of a verse within the context of the entire passage.

Focus on the facts of the passage, glean as much information as possible. You can start with the basics like 'What? When? How? Where? Why?' Probe further by asking detailed questions.

Who is speaking? What emotion are they expressing?
Who are they speaking to? Are they receptive or not?
Who is present?
What is happening?
What is the context? What was happening before and after?
What is God saying in this Scripture?
What is the main Truth?
Where is this taking place?
When is this taking place?
What caught your attention in what you read?

Ask the Holy Spirit to teach you. Write down the observations that helped you to understand the passage that you read. What resonated with you?

Remember, the Word of God is meant to be personal. It is God's love letter to you. When you study always be looking for the nugget that Jesus wants to work into your life.

Give me understanding, and I shall keep Your law;
Indeed, I shall observe it with my whole heart.
- Psalm 119:34

Reflecting
step three

Reflecting on the Scriptures is where the supernatural happens! Picture Jesus holding your face in His hands. He is looking deeply into your eyes and into your soul. He knows exactly what you need. He knows your hurts, hidden pain, and every broken piece of you. He knows your deep longings and all the desires of your heart. He knows your frustrations, your feelings of inadequacies, and thoughts of unworthiness. He is there holding you saying, "I love you. I've got this. You are going to be OK, more than OK. You are amazing and wonderful in my eyes. I have created you for a purpose, a great and eternal purpose, that we are going to fulfill together. Walk with Me, follow Me, call to Me, and I will show you great and mighty things that you do not know." How do I know He is saying these things to you? The Bible tells me so!

Your time of reflection on Scripture is your time to personally encounter Jesus. He is deeply in love with you. He is pursuing you and calling you into a deeper relationship with Him. He is growing you in grace and knowledge, and He is preparing you for what is ahead. Listen to what He is saying in the Word you have read. He is personally talking to you about something - LISTEN!

Life transformation happens through the time you spend with Jesus. What is it in your life that needs his kind touch, his grace, mercy, healing, or correction? Did this Scripture stir something in you? What difference can this Scripture make in your life? Write down your personal reflections in the space provided. Use your journal pages to elaborate on this.

. . . "Fear not, for I have redeemed you; I have called you by your name;
You are Mine." - Isaiah 43:1

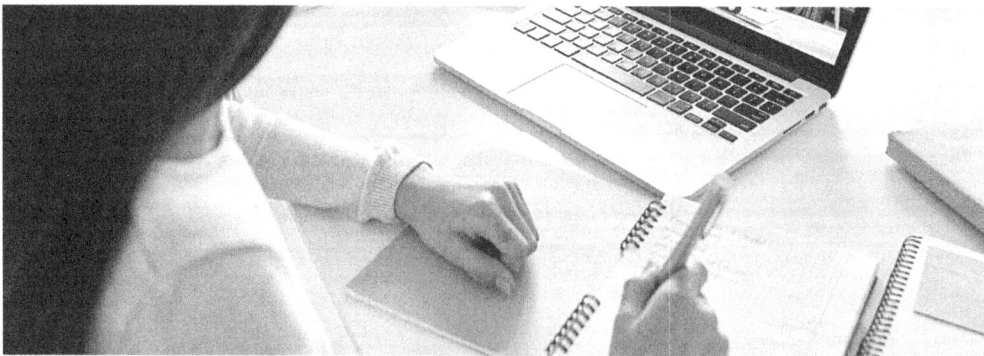

Doing
step four

"He who has My commandments and keeps them, it is he who loves Me. And he who loves Me will be loved by My Father, and I will love him and manifest Myself to him." - John 14:21

The Bible requires us to do something! It requires a response on our part. We first respond to God's love. If we do not believe and know that God loves us, it is almost impossible to respond to anything the Bible says. The greatest proof of His radical, reckless, never-ending love for us, is Jesus paying the penalty for our sins by suffering and dying on the cross and rising from the dead so we could spend an eternity in heaven with Him. That love requires a response from us individually. Once you know that God loves you, that He is for you; He has your best interests in mind; He will never leave you or forsake you, and that He is traveling along with you on this incredible journey called life; you can trust Him and obey Him. The doing is the obeying of the Word of God because of His great love for you, and now your love for Him. In John 14:21 Jesus promises that He will manifest, reveal Himself to you through your love and obedience. Amazing!

We are not just to read and hear the Word of God. We do something! The Word of God is also not just for our benefit; it is for the benefit of others. We do something! As Jesus followers we are called to be light in this dark world. We do something so men will see our good works and glorify our Father in heaven.

Every time you read the Bible, God is asking you to respond. He is asking you to do something. Ask yourself, "What is my response? How am I going to apply this to my life? What am I going to do?" Write your answer in the space provided.

But be doers of the word, and not hearers only, deceiving yourselves. James 1:22

Praying

step five

Prayer is entering God's presence where you are fully loved and accepted. The Disciples longed for this and asked Jesus, "Teach us to pray." The first thing Jesus does is teach them how to enter the throne room of God by addressing God as, "Our Father." You have a personal relationship with God as a loving, caring father has with his child. You have the right, as His child, to enter his throne of grace with boldness, where you will always obtain mercy and find grace in times of need.

The Lord's prayer is a guide given to us by Jesus where we can connect with God on a personal, intimate level. Prayer is a conversation with God that includes pouring out your heart and listening for His.

Every prayer page in your journal includes the Lord's prayer and a guide to focus you on each area that Jesus taught us to pray. You will be guided to praise God and surrender your will for His. Ask for your daily needs and the needs of others. Confess your sins and forgive those who have hurt you and sinned against you. Pray for guidance and deliverance from evil and end your prayer with worship. Pray like Jesus taught us to pray and you will increase your intimacy with God and see Him move mightily in your life.

Follow your prayer time by pouring out your heart to Him through journaling and writing down the words He speaks to you.

Let us therefore come boldly to the throne of grace, that we may obtain mercy and find grace to help in time of need. - Hebrews 4:16

Your prayer requests

Write out your prayer requests and record how God answers. *"Ask, and it will be given to you; seek, and you will find; knock, and it will be opened to you." - Matthew 7:7   Believe it!*

date	requests

date	answers

IN THIS MANNER, THEREFORE, PRAY:

OUR *Father* IN HEAVEN,

HALLOWED BE YOUR *name*.

YOUR *kingdom* COME.

Your will BE DONE

ON EARTH AS IT IS IN *heaven*.

Give us THIS DAY OUR *daily* BREAD.

AND *forgive* US OUR DEBTS,

AS WE *forgive* OUR DEBTORS.

AND DO NOT *lead* US INTO *temptation*,

BUT *deliver* US FROM THE *evil* ONE.

FOR *Yours* IS THE *kingdom* AND

THE *power* AND THE *glory* FOREVER.

AMEN.

MATTHEW 6:9-13

01 *Let not your heart be troubled*

- ⬡ Set my mind on Christ
- ⬡ Give Jesus my burdens
- ⬡ Meditate on Scripture
- ⬡ Read His Word
- ⬡ Align my thoughts
- ⬡ Talk with Jesus all day!
- ⬡ Give His love to others
- ⬡ Express Gratitude
- ⬡ Rejoice in this day

MORNING PRAYER

Casting all your care upon Him, for He cares for you.
1Peter 5:7

EVENING PRAISE

Praise the LORD! Oh, give thanks to the LORD,
for He is good! For His mercy endures forever.
Psalm 106:1

SCRIPTURE FOR TODAY

GRATITUDE JOURNAL

1.

2.

TODAY'S AFFIRMATION

3.

1. *I am a child of God.*
2.

Let not your heart be troubled; you believe in God, believe also in Me. - John 14:1

Open my eyes, that I may see Wondrous things from Your law. - Psalm 119:18

1 Word

2 Observing

3 Reflecting

4 Doing

Praying

Our Father in heaven,
Hallowed be Your name.
Your kingdom come.
Your will be done
on earth as it is in heaven.
Give us this day our daily bread.
And forgive us our debts,
as we forgive our debtors.
And do not lead us into temptation,
But deliver us from the evil one.
For Yours is the kingdom and
the power and the glory forever.
Amen.

MATTHEW 6:9-13

praise & HONOR YOUR
HEAVENLY FATHER

surrender YOUR WILL FOR HIS

ask FOR YOUR DAILY NEEDS & THE
NEEDS OF OTHERS.

confess YOUR SINS & RECEIVE
FORGIVENESS

forgive THOSE WHO HAVE
HURT YOU

guidance ASK FOR PROTECTION
& GUIDANCE AWAY
FROM TEMPTATIONS

deliverance ASK FOR DELIVERANCE
FROM THE SCHEMES
OF THE EVIL ONE

worship GOD AND BE GRATEFUL
FOR ALL HIS ATTRIBUTES

Bible Time
journal

BEHOLD WHAT MANNER OF *love* THE FATHER HAS BESTOWED ON US, THAT WE SHOULD BE CALLED *children of God* . . .

1 JOHN 3:1

"

He who has My commandments and keeps them, it is he who loves Me. And he who loves Me will be loved by My Father, and I will love him and manifest Myself to him.

- John 14:21

02 let not your heart be troubled

- ⬡ Set my mind on Christ
- ⬡ Give Jesus my burdens
- ⬡ Meditate on Scripture
- ⬡ Read His Word
- ⬡ Align my thoughts
- ⬡ Talk with Jesus all day!
- ⬡ Give His love to others
- ⬡ Express Gratitude
- ⬡ Rejoice in this day

MORNING PRAYER

Casting all your care upon Him, for He cares for you.
1Peter 5:7

EVENING PRAISE

Praise the LORD! Oh, give thanks to the LORD,
for He is good! For His mercy endures forever.
Psalm 106:1

SCRIPTURE FOR TODAY

GRATITUDE JOURNAL

1.

2.

TODAY'S AFFIRMATION

1. *I am loved.*

2.

3.

Let not your heart be troubled; you believe in God, believe also in Me. - John 14:1

Open my eyes, that I may see Wondrous things from Your law. - Psalm 119:18

1 Word

2 Observing

3 Reflecting

4 Doing

Praying

Our Father in heaven,
Hallowed be Your name.
Your kingdom come.
Your will be done
On earth as it is in heaven.
Give us this day our daily bread.
And forgive us our debts,
As we forgive our debtors.
And do not lead us into temptation.
But deliver us from the evil one.
For Yours is the kingdom and
the power and the glory forever.
Amen.

MATTHEW 6:9-13

praise & HONOR YOUR
HEAVENLY FATHER

surrender YOUR WILL FOR HIS

ask FOR YOUR DAILY NEEDS & THE
NEEDS OF OTHERS.

confess YOUR SINS & RECEIVE
FORGIVENESS

forgive THOSE WHO HAVE
HURT YOU

guidance ASK FOR PROTECTION
& GUIDANCE AWAY
FROM TEMPTATIONS

deliverance ASK FOR DELIVERANCE
FROM THE SCHEMES
OF THE EVIL ONE

worship GOD AND BE GRATEFUL
FOR ALL HIS ATTRIBUTES

Bible Time
journal

But his *delight* is in the law of the LORD,
and in His law he *meditates* day and night.

- Psalm 1:2

"

Yes,

I HAVE *loved* YOU WITH AN

everlasting love;

THEREFORE, WITH LOVINGKINDNESS

I HAVE *drawn you.*

JEREMIAH 31:3

03 let not your heart be troubled

Date:
S / M / T / W / T / F / S

- ⬡ Set my mind on Christ
- ⬡ Give Jesus my burdens
- ⬡ Meditate on Scripture

- ⬡ Read His Word
- ⬡ Align my thoughts
- ⬡ Talk with Jesus all day!

- ⬡ Give His love to others
- ⬡ Express Gratitude
- ⬡ Rejoice in this day

MORNING PRAYER

Casting all your care upon Him, for He cares for you.
1Peter 5:7

EVENING PRAISE

Praise the LORD! Oh, give thanks to the LORD,
for He is good! For His mercy endures forever.
Psalm 106:1

SCRIPTURE FOR TODAY

GRATITUDE JOURNAL

1.

2.

TODAY'S AFFIRMATION

1. *I am loved with an everlasting love.*

2.

3.

Let not your heart be troubled; you believe in God, believe also in Me. - John 14:1

Open my eyes, that I may see Wondrous things from Your law. - Psalm 119:18

1 Word

2 Observing

3 Reflecting

4 Doing

Praying

Our Father in heaven,
Hallowed be Your name.
Your kingdom come.
Your will be done
On earth as it is in heaven.
Give us this day our daily bread.
And forgive us our debts,
As we forgive our debtors.
And do not lead us into temptation,
But deliver us from the evil one.
For Yours is the kingdom and
The power and the glory forever.
Amen.

MATTHEW 6:9-13

praise & HONOR YOUR HEAVENLY FATHER

Surrender YOUR WILL FOR HIS

ask FOR YOUR DAILY NEEDS & THE NEEDS OF OTHERS.

confess YOUR SINS & RECEIVE FORGIVENESS

forgive THOSE WHO HAVE HURT YOU

guidance ASK FOR PROTECTION & GUIDANCE AWAY FROM TEMPTATIONS

deliverance ASK FOR DELIVERANCE FROM THE SCHEMES OF THE EVIL ONE

worship GOD AND BE GRATEFUL FOR ALL HIS ATTRIBUTES

Bible Time
journal

As the Father *loved* Me, I also have loved You; *abide* in My LOVE.

JOHN 15:9

"

Peace I leave with you,
My peace I give to you;
not as the world gives
do I give to you.
Let not your heart
be troubled, neither
let it be afraid.

– John 14:27

04 *let not your heart be troubled*

- ⬡ Set my mind on Christ
- ⬡ Give Jesus my burdens
- ⬡ Meditate on Scripture

- ⬡ Read His Word
- ⬡ Align my thoughts
- ⬡ Talk with Jesus all day!

- ⬡ Give His love to others
- ⬡ Express Gratitude
- ⬡ Rejoice in this day

MORNING PRAYER

Casting all your care upon Him, for He cares for you.
1Peter 5:7

EVENING PRAISE

Praise the LORD! Oh, give thanks to the LORD,
for He is good! For His mercy endures forever.
Psalm 106:1

SCRIPTURE FOR TODAY

GRATITUDE JOURNAL

1.

2.

TODAY'S AFFIRMATION

1. I have peace.

3.

2.

Let not your heart be troubled; you believe in God, believe also in Me. - John 14:1

Open my eyes, that I may see Wondrous things from Your law. - Psalm 119:18

1 Word

2 Observing

3 Reflecting

4 Doing

Praying

Our Father in heaven,
Hallowed be Your name.
Your kingdom come.
Your will be done
On earth as it is in heaven.
Give us this day our daily bread.
And forgive us our debts,
As we forgive our debtors.
And do not lead us into temptation.
But deliver us from the evil one.
For Yours is the kingdom and
the power and the glory forever.
Amen.

MATTHEW 6:9-13

praise & HONOR YOUR
HEAVENLY FATHER

surrender YOUR WILL FOR HIS

ask FOR YOUR DAILY NEEDS & THE
NEEDS OF OTHERS.

confess YOUR SINS & RECEIVE
FORGIVENESS

forgive THOSE WHO HAVE
HURT YOU

guidance ASK FOR PROTECTION
& GUIDANCE AWAY
FROM TEMPTATIONS

deliverance ASK FOR DELIVERANCE
FROM THE SCHEMES
OF THE EVIL ONE

worship GOD AND BE GRATEFUL
FOR ALL HIS ATTRIBUTES

Bible Time
journal

GREAT *peace* HAVE THOSE WHO *love* YOUR LAW.
AND NOTHING CAUSES THEM TO *stumble.*

. - PSALM 119:165

"

These things I have spoken to
you that My joy may remain in
you and that your joy may be full.
This is My commandment,
that you love one another as
I have loved you.

- John 15:11-12

05 let not your heart be troubled

Date:
S / M / T / W / T / F / S

BELIEVE

- Set my mind on Christ
- Give Jesus my burdens
- Meditate on Scripture
- Read His Word
- Align my thoughts
- Talk with Jesus all day!
- Give His love to others
- Express Gratitude
- Rejoice in this day

MORNING PRAYER

Casting all your care upon Him, for He cares for you.
1Peter 5:7

EVENING PRAISE

Praise the LORD! Oh, give thanks to the LORD,
for He is good! For His mercy endures forever.
Psalm 106:1

SCRIPTURE FOR TODAY

GRATITUDE JOURNAL

1.

2.

3.

TODAY'S AFFIRMATION

1. *I have fullness of joy.*

2.

Let not your heart be troubled; you believe in God, believe also in Me. - John 14:1

Open my eyes, that I may see Wondrous things from Your law. - Psalm 119:18

1 Word

2 Observing

3 Reflecting

4 Doing

Praying

Our Father in heaven,
Hallowed be Your name.
Your kingdom come.
Your will be done
On earth as it is in heaven.
Give us this day our daily bread.
And forgive us our debts,
As we forgive our debtors.
And do not lead us into temptation,
But deliver us from the evil one.
For Yours is the kingdom and
the power and the glory forever.
Amen.

MATTHEW 6:9-13

praise & HONOR YOUR
HEAVENLY FATHER

surrender YOUR WILL FOR HIS

ask FOR YOUR DAILY NEEDS & THE
NEEDS OF OTHERS.

confess YOUR SINS & RECEIVE
FORGIVENESS

forgive THOSE WHO HAVE
HURT YOU

guidance ASK FOR PROTECTION
& GUIDANCE AWAY
FROM TEMPTATIONS

deliverance ASK FOR DELIVERANCE
FROM THE SCHEMES
OF THE EVIL ONE

worship GOD AND BE GRATEFUL
FOR ALL HIS ATTRIBUTES

Bible Time
journal

I WILL BE *glad* AND *rejoice* IN YOU; I WILL *sing praise* TO YOUR NAME, O MOST HIGH.

. - PSALM 9:2

"

AND *above* ALL THINGS

HAVE *fervent* LOVE

FOR *one another*

FOR "LOVE WILL *cover*

A *multitude* OF SINS"

1 PETER 4:8

06 *let not your heart be troubled*

- Set my mind on Christ
- Give Jesus my burdens
- Meditate on Scripture
- Read His Word
- Align my thoughts
- Talk with Jesus all day!
- Give His love to others
- Express Gratitude
- Rejoice in this day

MORNING PRAYER

Casting all your care upon Him, for He cares for you.
1Peter 5:7

EVENING PRAISE

Praise the LORD! Oh, give thanks to the LORD,
for He is good! For His mercy endures forever.
Psalm 106:1

SCRIPTURE FOR TODAY

GRATITUDE JOURNAL

1.

2.

TODAY'S AFFIRMATION

1. *I have fervent love for others.*

3.

2.

Let not your heart be troubled; you believe in God, believe also in Me. - John 14:1

Open my eyes, that I may see Wondrous things from Your law. - Psalm 119:18

1 Word

2 Observing

3 Reflecting

4 Doing

Praying

Our Father in heaven,
Hallowed be Your name.
Your kingdom come.
Your will be done
On earth as it is in heaven.
Give us this day our daily bread.
And forgive us our debts,
As we forgive our debtors.
And do not lead us into temptation,
But deliver us from the evil one.
For Yours is the kingdom and
the power and the glory forever.
Amen.

MATTHEW 6:9-13

praise & HONOR YOUR
HEAVENLY FATHER

surrender YOUR WILL FOR HIS

ask FOR YOUR DAILY NEEDS & THE
NEEDS OF OTHERS.

confess YOUR SINS & RECEIVE
FORGIVENESS

forgive THOSE WHO HAVE
HURT YOU

guidance ASK FOR PROTECTION
& GUIDANCE AWAY
FROM TEMPTATIONS

deliverance ASK FOR DELIVERANCE
FROM THE SCHEMES
OF THE EVIL ONE

worship GOD AND BE GRATEFUL
FOR ALL HIS ATTRIBUTES

Bible Time journal

BY THIS ALL WILL *know* THAT YOU ARE MY *disciples* IF YOU HAVE *love.* FOR ONE ANOTHER.

- JOHN 13:35

The entirety of Your word

is truth

And every one of

Your righteous judgments

endures forever.

- Psalm 119:160

07 let not your heart be troubled

- ⬢ Set my mind on Christ
- ⬢ Give Jesus my burdens
- ⬢ Meditate on Scripture
- ⬢ Read His Word
- ⬢ Align my thoughts
- ⬢ Talk with Jesus all day!
- ⬢ Give His love to others
- ⬢ Express Gratitude
- ⬢ Rejoice in this day

MORNING PRAYER

*Casting all your care upon Him, for He cares for you.
1Peter 5:7*

EVENING PRAISE

*Praise the LORD! Oh, give thanks to the LORD,
for He is good! For His mercy endures forever.
Psalm 106:1*

SCRIPTURE FOR TODAY

GRATITUDE JOURNAL

1.

2.

TODAY'S AFFIRMATION

1. *I have the Truth. God's Word is truth.*

3.

2.

Let not your heart be troubled; you believe in God, believe also in Me. - John 14:1

Open my eyes, that I may see Wondrous things from Your law. - Psalm 119:18

1 Word

2 Observing

3 Reflecting

4 Doing

Praying

Our Father in heaven,
Hallowed be Your name.
Your kingdom come.
Your will be done
On earth as it is in heaven.
Give us this day our daily bread.
And forgive us our debts,
As we forgive our debtors.
And do not lead us into temptation,
But deliver us from the evil one.
For Yours is the kingdom and
The power and the glory forever.
Amen.

MATTHEW 6:9-13

praise & HONOR YOUR HEAVENLY FATHER

surrender YOUR WILL FOR HIS

ask FOR YOUR DAILY NEEDS & THE NEEDS OF OTHERS.

confess YOUR SINS & RECEIVE FORGIVENESS

forgive THOSE WHO HAVE HURT YOU

guidance ASK FOR PROTECTION & GUIDANCE AWAY FROM TEMPTATIONS

deliverance ASK FOR DELIVERANCE FROM THE SCHEMES OF THE EVIL ONE

worship GOD AND BE GRATEFUL FOR ALL HIS ATTRIBUTES

Bible Time
journal

I AM THE *way* THE *truth* THE *life*

NO ONE COMES TO THE FATHER EXCEPT THROUGH *Me.*

JOHN 14:6

LET YOUR *light*
SO
shine BEFORE MEN,

THAT THEY MAY *see*

YOUR
good works AND

glorify YOUR *Father*

IN HEAVEN.

- MATTHEW 5:16

08 *let not your heart be troubled*

Date:
S / M / T / W / T / F / S

- ⬡ Set my mind on Christ
- ⬡ Give Jesus my burdens
- ⬡ Meditate on Scripture
- ⬡ Read His Word
- ⬡ Align my thoughts
- ⬡ Talk with Jesus all day!
- ⬡ Give His love to others
- ⬡ Express Gratitude
- ⬡ Rejoice in this day

MORNING PRAYER

Casting all your care upon Him, for He cares for you.
1Peter 5:7

EVENING PRAISE

Praise the LORD! Oh, give thanks to the LORD,
for He is good! For His mercy endures forever.
Psalm 106:1

SCRIPTURE FOR TODAY

GRATITUDE JOURNAL

1.

2.

TODAY'S AFFIRMATION

1. *I have the light of Jesus in me. Go shine!*

2.

3.

Let not your heart be troubled; you believe in God, believe also in Me. - John 14:1

Open my eyes, that I may see Wondrous things from Your law. - Psalm 119:18

1 Word

2 Observing

3 Reflecting

4 Doing

Praying

Our Father in heaven,
Hallowed be Your name.
Your kingdom come.
Your will be done
On earth as it is in heaven.
Give us this day our daily bread.
And forgive us our debts,
As we forgive our debtors.
And do not lead us into temptation,
But deliver us from the evil one.
For Yours is the kingdom and
the power and the glory forever.
Amen.

MATTHEW 6:9-13

praise & HONOR YOUR HEAVENLY FATHER

surrender YOUR WILL FOR HIS

ask FOR YOUR DAILY NEEDS & THE NEEDS OF OTHERS.

confess YOUR SINS & RECEIVE FORGIVENESS

forgive THOSE WHO HAVE HURT YOU

guidance ASK FOR PROTECTION & GUIDANCE AWAY FROM TEMPTATIONS

deliverance ASK FOR DELIVERANCE FROM THE SCHEMES OF THE EVIL ONE

worship GOD AND BE GRATEFUL FOR ALL HIS ATTRIBUTES

Bible Time
journal

YOU ARE THE *light* OF THE *world.* A CITY
THAT IS SET ON A HILL, THAT CANNOT BE *hidden.*

- MATTHEW 5:14

" But I say to you, love your enemies, bless those who curse you, do good to those who hate you, and pray for those who spitefully use you and persecute you.

- Matthew 5:44

09 *let not your heart be troubled*

Date:
S / M / T / W / T / F / S

BELIEVE

- Set my mind on Christ
- Give Jesus my burdens
- Meditate on Scripture
- Read His Word
- Align my thoughts
- Talk with Jesus all day!
- Give His love to others
- Express Gratitude
- Rejoice in this day

MORNING PRAYER

Casting all your care upon Him, for He cares for you.
1Peter 5:7

EVENING PRAISE

Praise the LORD! Oh, give thanks to the LORD,
for He is good! For His mercy endures forever.
Psalm 106:1

SCRIPTURE FOR TODAY

GRATITUDE JOURNAL

1.

2.

TODAY'S AFFIRMATION

1. *I am kind. I am merciful.*
2.

3.

Let not your heart be troubled; you believe in God, believe also in Me. - John 14:1

Open my eyes, that I may see Wondrous things from Your law. - Psalm 119:18

1 Word

2 Observing

3 Reflecting

4 Doing

Praying

Our Father in heaven,
Hallowed be Your name.
Your kingdom come.
Your will be done
on earth as it is in heaven.
Give us this day our daily bread.
And forgive us our debts,
as we forgive our debtors.
And do not lead us into temptation,
But deliver us from the evil one.
For Yours is the kingdom and
the power and the glory forever.
Amen.

MATTHEW 6:9-13

praise & HONOR YOUR
HEAVENLY FATHER

surrender YOUR WILL FOR HIS

ask FOR YOUR DAILY NEEDS & THE
NEEDS OF OTHERS.

confess YOUR SINS & RECEIVE
FORGIVENESS

forgive THOSE WHO HAVE
HURT YOU

guidance ASK FOR PROTECTION
& GUIDANCE AWAY
FROM TEMPTATIONS

deliverance ASK FOR DELIVERANCE
FROM THE SCHEMES
OF THE EVIL ONE

worship GOD AND BE GRATEFUL
FOR ALL HIS ATTRIBUTES

Bible Time
journal

...FOR HE IS *kind* TO THE UNTHANKFUL AND EVIL..

THEREFORE BE *merciful* AS YOUR FATHER

ALSO IS *merciful.*

- LUKE 6:35-36

> Then Jesus said to His disciples, "If anyone desires to come after Me, let him deny himself, and take up his cross, and follow Me."

— Matthew 16:24

10 let not your heart be troubled

Date:
S / M / T / W / T / F / S

- Set my mind on Christ
- Give Jesus my burdens
- Meditate on Scripture
- Read His Word
- Align my thoughts
- Talk with Jesus all day!
- Give His love to others
- Express Gratitude
- Rejoice in this day

MORNING PRAYER

Casting all your care upon Him, for He cares for you.
1Peter 5:7

EVENING PRAISE

Praise the LORD! Oh, give thanks to the LORD,
for He is good! For His mercy endures forever.
Psalm 106:1

SCRIPTURE FOR TODAY

GRATITUDE JOURNAL

1.

2.

TODAY'S AFFIRMATION

3.

1. I am a Christ follower. I deny myself.
2.

Let not your heart be troubled; you believe in God, believe also in Me. - John 14:1

Open my eyes, that I may see Wondrous things from Your law. - Psalm 119:18

1 Word

2 Observing

3 Reflecting

4 Doing

Praying

Our Father in heaven,
Hallowed be Your name.
Your kingdom come.
Your will be done
On earth as it is in heaven.
Give us this day our daily bread.
And forgive us our debts,
As we forgive our debtors.
And do not lead us into temptation,
But deliver us from the evil one.
For Yours is the kingdom and
the power and the glory forever.
Amen.

MATTHEW 6:9-13

praise & HONOR YOUR HEAVENLY FATHER

surrender YOUR WILL FOR HIS

ask FOR YOUR DAILY NEEDS & THE NEEDS OF OTHERS.

confess YOUR SINS & RECEIVE FORGIVENESS

forgive THOSE WHO HAVE HURT YOU

guidance ASK FOR PROTECTION & GUIDANCE AWAY FROM TEMPTATIONS

deliverance ASK FOR DELIVERANCE FROM THE SCHEMES OF THE EVIL ONE

worship GOD AND BE GRATEFUL FOR ALL HIS ATTRIBUTES

Bible Time
journal

MY *sheep* HEAR MY *voice*, AND I *know* THEM, AND THEY *follow* ME.

- JOHN 10:27

"

Do not lay up for yourselves treasures on earth, where moth and rust destroy and where thieves break in and steal but lay up for yourselves treasures in heaven, where neither moth nor rust destroys and where thieves do not break in and steal. For where your treasure is, there your heart will be also.

- Matthew 6:19-21

11 *let not your heart be troubled*

- ⬡ Set my mind on Christ
- ⬡ Give Jesus my burdens
- ⬡ Meditate on Scripture

- ⬡ Read His Word
- ⬡ Align my thoughts
- ⬡ Talk with Jesus all day!

- ⬡ Give His love to others
- ⬡ Express Gratitude
- ⬡ Rejoice in this day

MORNING PRAYER

Casting all your care upon Him, for He cares for you.
1Peter 5:7

EVENING PRAISE

Praise the LORD! Oh, give thanks to the LORD, for He is good! For His mercy endures forever.
Psalm 106:1

SCRIPTURE FOR TODAY

GRATITUDE JOURNAL

1.

2.

TODAY'S AFFIRMATION

1. *I lay up treasures in heaven.*

2.

3.

Let not your heart be troubled; you believe in God, believe also in Me. - John 14:1

Open my eyes, that I may see Wondrous things from Your law. - Psalm 119:18

1 Word

2 Observing

3 Reflecting

4 Doing

Praying

Our Father in heaven,
Hallowed be Your name.
Your kingdom come.
Your will be done
On earth as it is in heaven.
Give us this day our daily bread.
And forgive us our debts,
As we forgive our debtors.
And do not lead us into temptation,
But deliver us from the evil one.
For Yours is the kingdom and
the power and the glory forever.
Amen.

MATTHEW 6:9-13

praise & HONOR YOUR HEAVENLY FATHER

Surrender YOUR WILL FOR HIS

ask FOR YOUR DAILY NEEDS & THE NEEDS OF OTHERS.

confess YOUR SINS & RECEIVE FORGIVENESS

forgive THOSE WHO HAVE HURT YOU

guidance ASK FOR PROTECTION & GUIDANCE AWAY FROM TEMPTATIONS

deliverance ASK FOR DELIVERANCE FROM THE SCHEMES OF THE EVIL ONE

worship GOD AND BE GRATEFUL FOR ALL HIS ATTRIBUTES

Bible Time
journal

I *rejoice* AT YOUR WORD
AS ONE WHO *finds* GREAT *treasure*.

- PSALM 119:162

" But seek first the kingdom of God and His righteousness, and all these things shall be added to you. Therefore do not worry about tomorrow, for tomorrow will worry about its own things. Sufficient for the day is its own trouble. - Matthew 6:33-34

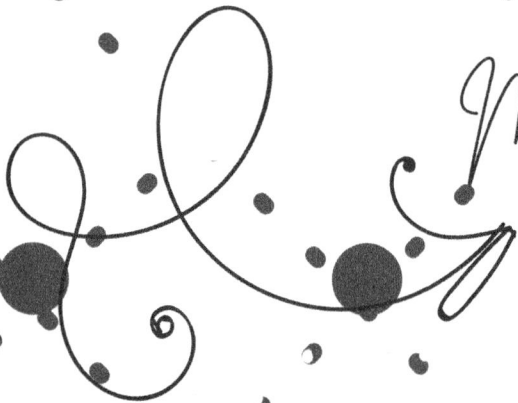

12 *Let not your heart be troubled*

Date:
S / M / T / W / T / F / S

BELIEVE

- ⬡ Set my mind on Christ
- ⬡ Give Jesus my burdens
- ⬡ Meditate on Scripture
- ⬡ Read His Word
- ⬡ Align my thoughts
- ⬡ Talk with Jesus all day!
- ⬡ Give His love to others
- ⬡ Express Gratitude
- ⬡ Rejoice in this day

MORNING PRAYER

Casting all your care upon Him, for He cares for you.
1Peter 5:7

EVENING PRAISE

Praise the LORD! Oh, give thanks to the LORD, for He is good! For His mercy endures forever.
Psalm 106:1

SCRIPTURE FOR TODAY

GRATITUDE JOURNAL

1.

2.

TODAY'S AFFIRMATION

1. *I seek first the kingdom of God.*

2.

3.

Let not your heart be troubled; you believe in God, believe also in Me. - John 14:1

Open my eyes, that I may see Wondrous things from Your law. - Psalm 119:18

1 Word

2 Observing

3 Reflecting

4 Doing

Praying

Our Father in heaven,
Hallowed be Your name.
Your kingdom come.
Your will be done
On earth as it is in heaven.
Give us this day our daily bread.
And forgive us our debts,
As we forgive our debtors.
And do not lead us into temptation,
But deliver us from the evil one.
For Yours is the kingdom and
the power and the glory forever.
Amen.

MATTHEW 6:9-13

praise & HONOR YOUR
HEAVENLY FATHER

surrender YOUR WILL FOR HIS

ask FOR YOUR DAILY NEEDS & THE
NEEDS OF OTHERS.

confess YOUR SINS & RECEIVE
FORGIVENESS

forgive THOSE WHO HAVE
HURT YOU

guidance ASK FOR PROTECTION
& GUIDANCE AWAY
FROM TEMPTATIONS

deliverance ASK FOR DELIVERANCE
FROM THE SCHEMES
OF THE EVIL ONE

worship GOD AND BE GRATEFUL
FOR ALL HIS ATTRIBUTES

Bible Time
journal

NOT THAT I SPEAK IN REGARD TO *need*, FOR i HAVE *learned*, IN WHATEVER STATE I AM, TO BE *content.*

- PHILIPPIANS 4:11

"

These things I have spoken
to you, that in Me
you may have peace.
In the world you
will have tribulation;
but be of good cheer,
I have overcome the world."

— John 16:33

13 Let not your heart be troubled

Date:
S / M / T / W / T / F / S

- Set my mind on Christ
- Give Jesus my burdens
- Meditate on Scripture
- Read His Word
- Align my thoughts
- Talk with Jesus all day!
- Give His love to others
- Express Gratitude
- Rejoice in this day

MORNING PRAYER

Casting all your care upon Him, for He cares for you.
1Peter 5:7

EVENING PRAISE

Praise the LORD! Oh, give thanks to the LORD,
for He is good! For His mercy endures forever.
Psalm 106:1

SCRIPTURE FOR TODAY

GRATITUDE JOURNAL

1.

2.

TODAY'S AFFIRMATION

1. *I am of good cheer.*
2.

3.

Let not your heart be troubled; you believe in God, believe also in Me. - John 14:1

Open my eyes, that I may see Wondrous things from Your law. - Psalm 119:18

1 Word

2 Observing

3 Reflecting

4 Doing

Praying

Our Father in heaven,
Hallowed be Your name.
Your kingdom come.
Your will be done
on earth as it is in heaven.
Give us this day our daily bread.
And forgive us our debts,
As we forgive our debtors.
And do not lead us into temptation,
But deliver us from the evil one.
For Yours is the kingdom and
the power and the glory forever.
Amen.

Matthew 6

praise & honor your
heavenly father

Surrender your will for His

ask for your daily needs & the
needs of others.

confess your sins & receive
forgiveness

forgive those who have
hurt you

guidance ask for protection
& guidance away
from temptations

deliverance ask for deliverance
from the schemes
of the evil one

worship god and be grateful
for all his attributes

Bible Time
journal

FOR WHATEVER IS BORN OF GOD OVERCOMES THE *world*.

AND THIS IS THE *victory* THAT HAS *overcome*

THE WORLD - - *our faith*. - 1JOHN 5:4 1

"

HAVE I NOT COMMANDED YOU?

BE *strong* AND OF GOOD

courage DO NOT BE *afraid*

NOR BE *dismayed*

FOR THE LORD YOUR GOD

IS WITH YOU

wherever you go.

JOSHUA 1:9

14 let not your heart be troubled

Date:
S / M / T / W / T / F / S

- ⬡ Set my mind on Christ
- ⬡ Give Jesus my burdens
- ⬡ Meditate on Scripture
- ⬡ Read His Word
- ⬡ Align my thoughts
- ⬡ Talk with Jesus all day!
- ⬡ Give His love to others
- ⬡ Express Gratitude
- ⬡ Rejoice in this day

MORNING PRAYER

Casting all your care upon Him, for He cares for you.
1Peter 5:7

EVENING PRAISE

Praise the LORD! Oh, give thanks to the LORD,
for He is good! For His mercy endures forever.
Psalm 106:1

SCRIPTURE FOR TODAY

GRATITUDE JOURNAL

1.

2.

TODAY'S AFFIRMATION

1. I am strong and courageous.

2.

3.

Let not your heart be troubled; you believe in God, believe also in Me. - John 14:1

Open my eyes, that I may see Wondrous things from Your law. - Psalm 119:18

1 Word

2 Observing

3 Reflecting

4 Doing

Praying

Our Father in heaven,
Hallowed be Your name.
Your kingdom come.
Your will be done
on earth as it is in heaven.
Give us this day our daily bread.
And forgive us our debts,
as we forgive our debtors.
And do not lead us into temptation,
but deliver us from the evil one.
For Yours is the kingdom and
the power and the glory forever.
Amen.

MATTHEW 6:9-13

praise & HONOR YOUR HEAVENLY FATHER

surrender YOUR WILL FOR HIS

ask FOR YOUR DAILY NEEDS & THE NEEDS OF OTHERS.

confess YOUR SINS & RECEIVE FORGIVENESS

forgive THOSE WHO HAVE HURT YOU

guidance ASK FOR PROTECTION & GUIDANCE AWAY FROM TEMPTATIONS

deliverance ASK FOR DELIVERANCE FROM THE SCHEMES OF THE EVIL ONE

worship GOD AND BE GRATEFUL FOR ALL HIS ATTRIBUTES

Bible Time
journal

DO NOT *fear* LITTLE FLOCK, FOR IT IS YOUR FATHER'S GOOD *pleasure*. TO GIVE YOU THE *kingdom*..

- LUKE 12:32

"

I have been crucified with Christ;
it is no longer I who live,
but Christ lives in me;
and the life which I now live in the
flesh I live by faith in the
Son of God, who loved me
and gave Himself for me.

— Galatians 2:20

15

let not your heart be troubled

Date:
S / M / T / W / T / F / S

- ⬡ Set my mind on Christ
- ⬡ Give Jesus my burdens
- ⬡ Meditate on Scripture

- ⬡ Read His Word
- ⬡ Align my thoughts
- ⬡ Talk with Jesus all day!

- ⬡ Give His love to others
- ⬡ Express Gratitude
- ⬡ Rejoice in this day

MORNING PRAYER

Casting all your care upon Him, for He cares for you.
1Peter 5:7

EVENING PRAISE

Praise the LORD! Oh, give thanks to the LORD,
for He is good! For His mercy endures forever.
Psalm 106:1

SCRIPTURE FOR TODAY

GRATITUDE JOURNAL

1.

2.

TODAY'S AFFIRMATION

1. **Christ lives in me.**
2.

3.

Let not your heart be troubled; you believe in God, believe also in Me. - John 14:1

Open my eyes, that I may see Wondrous things from Your law. - Psalm 119:18

1 Word

2 Observing

3 Reflecting

4 Doing

Praying

Our Father in heaven,
Hallowed be Your name.
Your kingdom come.
Your will be done
On earth as it is in heaven.
Give us this day our daily bread.
And forgive us our debts,
As we forgive our debtors.
And do not lead us into temptation,
But deliver us from the evil one.
For Yours is the kingdom and
the power and the glory forever.
Amen.

MATTHEW 6:9-13

praise & HONOR YOUR
HEAVENLY FATHER

Surrender YOUR WILL FOR HIS

ask FOR YOUR DAILY NEEDS & THE
NEEDS OF OTHERS.

confess YOUR SINS & RECEIVE
FORGIVENESS

forgive THOSE WHO HAVE
HURT YOU

guidance ASK FOR PROTECTION
& GUIDANCE AWAY
FROM TEMPTATIONS

deliverance ASK FOR DELIVERANCE
FROM THE SCHEMES
OF THE EVIL ONE

worship GOD AND BE GRATEFUL
FOR ALL HIS ATTRIBUTES

Bible Time
journal

FOR WE WALK BY *faith*, NOT BY *sight*.

- 2CORINTHIANS 5:7

"

Now to him who is able

to do

exceedingly abundantly

above all that we ask or think,

according to the *power*

that works in us,

Ephesians 3:20

16 Let not your heart be troubled

Date:
S / M / T / W / T / F / S

- Set my mind on Christ
- Give Jesus my burdens
- Meditate on Scripture

- Read His Word
- Align my thoughts
- Talk with Jesus all day!

- Give His love to others
- Express Gratitude
- Rejoice in this day

MORNING PRAYER

Casting all your care upon Him, for He cares for you.
1Peter 5:7

EVENING PRAISE

Praise the LORD! Oh, give thanks to the LORD,
for He is good! For His mercy endures forever.
Psalm 106:1

SCRIPTURE FOR TODAY

GRATITUDE JOURNAL

1.

2.

TODAY'S AFFIRMATION

1. *There is power working in me.*

2.

3.

Let not your heart be troubled; you believe in God, believe also in Me. - John 14:1

Open my eyes, that I may see Wondrous things from Your law. - Psalm 119:18

1 Word

2 Observing

3 Reflecting

4 Doing

Praying

Our Father in heaven,
Hallowed be Your name.
Your kingdom come.
Your will be done
On earth as it is in heaven.
Give us this day our daily bread.
And forgive us our debts,
As we forgive our debtors.
And do not lead us into temptation,
But deliver us from the evil one.
For Yours is the kingdom and
The power and the glory forever.
Amen.

MATTHEW 6:9-13

praise & HONOR YOUR HEAVENLY FATHER

surrender YOUR WILL FOR HIS

ask FOR YOUR DAILY NEEDS & THE NEEDS OF OTHERS.

confess YOUR SINS & RECEIVE FORGIVENESS

forgive THOSE WHO HAVE HURT YOU

guidance ASK FOR PROTECTION & GUIDANCE AWAY FROM TEMPTATIONS

deliverance ASK FOR DELIVERANCE FROM THE SCHEMES OF THE EVIL ONE

worship GOD AND BE GRATEFUL FOR ALL HIS ATTRIBUTES

Bible Time
journal

I HAVE COME THAT THEY MAY HAVE *life*, AND THAT THEY MAY HAVE IT MORE *abundantly*. JOHN 10:10

"

Be anxious for nothing, but in everything by prayer and supplication, with thanksgiving, let your requests be made known to God; and the peace of God, which surpasses all understanding, will guard your hearts and minds through Christ Jesus.

- Philippians 4:6-7

17 *Let not your heart be troubled*

- Set my mind on Christ
- Give Jesus my burdens
- Meditate on Scripture
- Read His Word
- Align my thoughts
- Talk with Jesus all day!
- Give His love to others
- Express Gratitude
- Rejoice in this day

MORNING PRAYER

Casting all your care upon Him, for He cares for you.
1Peter 5:7

EVENING PRAISE

*Praise the LORD! Oh, give thanks to the LORD,
for He is good! For His mercy endures forever.*
Psalm 106:1

SCRIPTURE FOR TODAY

GRATITUDE JOURNAL

1.

2.

3.

TODAY'S AFFIRMATION

1. *I am thankful.*
2.

Let not your heart be troubled; you believe in God, believe also in Me. - John 14:1

Open my eyes, that I may see Wondrous things from Your law. - Psalm 119:18

1 Word

2 Observing

3 Reflecting

4 Doing

Praying

Our Father in heaven,
Hallowed be Your name.
Your kingdom come.
Your will be done
On earth as it is in heaven.
Give us this day our daily bread.
And forgive us our debts,
As we forgive our debtors.
And do not lead us into temptation,
But deliver us from the evil one.
For Yours is the kingdom and
the power and the glory forever.
Amen.

MATTHEW 6:9-13

praise & HONOR YOUR
HEAVENLY FATHER

Surrender YOUR WILL FOR HIS

ask FOR YOUR DAILY NEEDS & THE
NEEDS OF OTHERS.

confess YOUR SINS & RECEIVE
FORGIVENESS

forgive THOSE WHO HAVE
HURT YOU

guidance ASK FOR PROTECTION
& GUIDANCE AWAY
FROM TEMPTATIONS

deliverance ASK FOR DELIVERANCE
FROM THE SCHEMES
OF THE EVIL ONE

worship GOD AND BE GRATEFUL
FOR ALL HIS ATTRIBUTES

Bible Time
journal

CALL TO ME, AND I WILL *answer* YOU, AND SHOW YOU

GREAT AND *mighty things* WHICH YOU DO NOT KNOW.

- JEREMIAH 33:3

"

Finally Brethren,

WHATEVER THINGS ARE *noble*

WHATEVER THINGS ARE *just*

WHATEVER THINGS ARE *pure*

WHATEVER THINGS ARE *lovely*

WHATEVER THINGS ARE OF *good report*

IF THERE IS ANY *virtue* AND IF

THERE IS ANYTHING *praise worthy*

meditate on these things.

PHILIPPIANS 4:8

18 *let not your heart be troubled*

- ⬢ Set my mind on Christ
- ⬢ Give Jesus my burdens
- ⬢ Meditate on Scripture
- ⬢ Read His Word
- ⬢ Align my thoughts
- ⬢ Talk with Jesus all day!
- ⬢ Give His love to others
- ⬢ Express Gratitude
- ⬢ Rejoice in this day

MORNING PRAYER

*Casting all your care upon Him, for He cares for you.
1Peter 5:7*

EVENING PRAISE

*Praise the LORD! Oh, give thanks to the LORD,
for He is good! For His mercy endures forever.
Psalm 106:1*

SCRIPTURE FOR TODAY

GRATITUDE JOURNAL

1.

2.

TODAY'S AFFIRMATION

1. *I focus my mind on good things.*

2.

3.

Let not your heart be troubled; you believe in God, believe also in Me. - John 14:1

Open my eyes, that I may see Wondrous things from Your law. - Psalm 119:18

1 Word

2 Observing

3 Reflecting

4 Doing

Praying

Our Father in heaven,
Hallowed be Your name.
Your kingdom come.
Your will be done
On earth as it is in heaven.
Give us this day our daily bread.
And forgive us our debts,
As we forgive our debtors.
And do not lead us into temptation,
But deliver us from the evil one.
For Yours is the kingdom and
the power and the glory forever.
Amen.

MATTHEW 6:9-13

praise & HONOR YOUR HEAVENLY FATHER

surrender YOUR WILL FOR HIS

ask FOR YOUR DAILY NEEDS & THE NEEDS OF OTHERS.

confess YOUR SINS & RECEIVE FORGIVENESS

forgive THOSE WHO HAVE HURT YOU

guidance ASK FOR PROTECTION & GUIDANCE AWAY FROM TEMPTATIONS

deliverance ASK FOR DELIVERANCE FROM THE SCHEMES OF THE EVIL ONE

worship GOD AND BE GRATEFUL FOR ALL HIS ATTRIBUTES

Bible Time
journal

BRINGING EVERY *thought* INTO *captivity* TO THE *obedience* OF *Christ.*

- 2CORINTHIANS 10:5

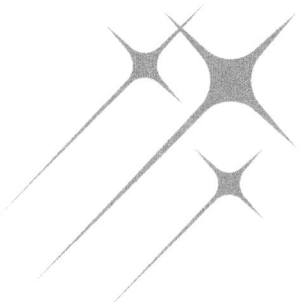

"

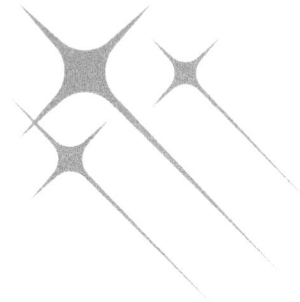

I WOULD HAVE LOST HEART, UNLESS I HAD BELIEVED THAT I WOULD SEE THE GOODNESS OF THE LORD IN THE LAND OF THE LIVING.

wait ON THE LORD;

BE OF good courage,

AND HE WILL

strenghten YOUR heart.

wait, I SAY, ON THE LORD!

- PSALM 27:13-14

19 let not your heart be troubled

Date:
S / M / T / W / T / F / S

⬡ Set my mind on Christ
⬡ Give Jesus my burdens
⬡ Meditate on Scripture

⬡ Read His Word
⬡ Align my thoughts
⬡ Talk with Jesus all day!

⬡ Give His love to others
⬡ Express Gratitude
⬡ Rejoice in this day

MORNING PRAYER

Casting all your care upon Him, for He cares for you.
1Peter 5:7

EVENING PRAISE

Praise the LORD! Oh, give thanks to the LORD,
for He is good! For His mercy endures forever.
Psalm 106:1

SCRIPTURE FOR TODAY

GRATITUDE JOURNAL

1.

2.

TODAY'S AFFIRMATION

1. *I wait on the Lord.*

2.

3.

Let not your heart be troubled; you believe in God, believe also in Me. - John 14:1

Open my eyes, that I may see Wondrous things from Your law. - Psalm 119:18

1 Word

2 Observing

3 Reflecting

4 Doing

Praying

Our Father in heaven,
Hallowed be Your name.
Your kingdom come.
Your will be done
on earth as it is in heaven.
Give us this day our daily bread.
And forgive us our debts,
as we forgive our debtors.
And do not lead us into temptation,
but deliver us from the evil one.
For Yours is the kingdom and
the power and the glory forever.
Amen.

MATTHEW 6:9-13

praise & honor your heavenly Father

Surrender your will for His

ask for your daily needs & the needs of others.

confess your sins & receive forgiveness

forgive those who have hurt you

guidance ask for protection & guidance away from temptations

deliverance ask for deliverance from the schemes of the evil one

worship God and be grateful for all His attributes

Bible Time
journal

BUT THOSE WHO *wait* ON THE LORD SHALL *renew* THEIR *strength.*
THEY SHALL MOUNT UP WITH WINGS LIKE *eagles.* THEY SHALL *run*
AND NOT BE *weary.* THEY SHALL *walk* AND NOT *faint.*

- ISAIAH 40:31

"

JESUS ANSWERED HIM,

THE FIRST OF ALL THE *commandments* IS

'HEAR O ISRAEL, THE LORD OUR GOD, THE LORD IS ONE. AND

YOU SHALL *love* THE LORD YOUR GOD WITH

all your heart, WITH *all your soul*, WITH

all your mind, AND WITH ALL *all your strength*.

THE FIRST COMMANDMENT. AND THE SECOND, LIKE IT, IS THIS:

You shall love,

YOUR *neighbor* AS *yourself*.

THEIR IS NO OTHER COMMANDMENT GREATER THAN THESE.

MARK 12:29-31

20 *let not your heart be troubled*

- ⬡ Set my mind on Christ
- ⬡ Give Jesus my burdens
- ⬡ Meditate on Scripture
- ⬡ Read His Word
- ⬡ Align my thoughts
- ⬡ Talk with Jesus all day!
- ⬡ Give His love to others
- ⬡ Express Gratitude
- ⬡ Rejoice in this day

MORNING PRAYER

Casting all your care upon Him, for He cares for you.
1Peter 5:7

EVENING PRAISE

Praise the LORD! Oh, give thanks to the LORD,
for He is good! For His mercy endures forever.
Psalm 106:1

SCRIPTURE FOR TODAY

GRATITUDE JOURNAL

1.

2.

TODAY'S AFFIRMATION

1. *I love God and I love others.*
2.

3.

Let not your heart be troubled; you believe in God, believe also in Me. - John 14:1

Open my eyes, that I may see Wondrous things from Your law. - Psalm 119:18

1 Word

2 Observing

3 Reflecting

4 Doing

Praying

Our Father in heaven,
Hallowed be Your name.
Your kingdom come.
Your will be done
On earth as it is in heaven.
Give us this day our daily bread.
And forgive us our debts,
As we forgive our debtors.
And do not lead us into temptation.
But deliver us from the evil one.
For Yours is the kingdom and
the power and the glory forever.
Amen.

MATTHEW 6:9-13

praise & HONOR YOUR HEAVENLY FATHER

Surrender YOUR WILL FOR HIS

ask FOR YOUR DAILY NEEDS & THE NEEDS OF OTHERS.

confess YOUR SINS & RECEIVE FORGIVENESS

forgive THOSE WHO HAVE HURT YOU

guidance ASK FOR PROTECTION & GUIDANCE AWAY FROM TEMPTATIONS

deliverance ASK FOR DELIVERANCE FROM THE SCHEMES OF THE EVIL ONE

worship GOD AND BE GRATEFUL FOR ALL HIS ATTRIBUTES

Bible Time
journal

THEREFORE TAKE *careful heed* TO YOURSELVES, THAT YOU *love* THE LORD YOUR GOD. - JOSHUA 23:11

"

Give to the LORD
the glory due His name;
Bring an offering, and come
before Him. Oh, worship
THE LORD
in the beauty of holiness!

- 1Chronicles 16:29

21 *let not your heart be troubled*

- ⬡ Set my mind on Christ
- ⬡ Give Jesus my burdens
- ⬡ Meditate on Scripture

- ⬡ Read His Word
- ⬡ Align my thoughts
- ⬡ Talk with Jesus all day!

- ⬡ Give His love to others
- ⬡ Express Gratitude
- ⬡ Rejoice in this day

MORNING PRAYER

Casting all your care upon Him, for He cares for you.
1Peter 5:7

EVENING PRAISE

Praise the LORD! Oh, give thanks to the LORD,
for He is good! For His mercy endures forever.
Psalm 106:1

SCRIPTURE FOR TODAY

GRATITUDE JOURNAL

1.

2.

TODAY'S AFFIRMATION

1. *I worship the Lord.*

2.

3.

Let not your heart be troubled; you believe in God, believe also in Me. - John 14:1

Open my eyes, that I may see Wondrous things from Your law. - Psalm 119:18

1 Word

2 Observing

3 Reflecting

4 Doing

Praying

Our Father in heaven,
Hallowed be Your name.
Your kingdom come.
Your will be done
On earth as it is in heaven.
Give us this day our daily bread.
And forgive us our debts,
As we forgive our debtors.
And do not lead us into temptation,
But deliver us from the evil one.
For Yours is the kingdom and
the power and the glory forever.
Amen.

MATTHEW 6:9-13

praise & HONOR YOUR
HEAVENLY FATHER

Surrender YOUR WILL FOR His

ask FOR YOUR DAILY NEEDS & THE
NEEDS OF OTHERS.

confess YOUR SINS & RECEIVE
FORGIVENESS

forgive THOSE WHO HAVE
HURT YOU

guidance ASK FOR PROTECTION
& GUIDANCE AWAY
FROM TEMPTATIONS

deliverance ASK FOR DELIVERANCE
FROM THE SCHEMES
OF THE EVIL ONE

worship GOD AND BE GRATEFUL
FOR ALL HIS ATTRIBUTES

Bible Time
journal

OH, *magnify* THE LORD *with me*.

AND LET US, *exalt* HIS NAME *together*.

– Psalm 34:3

"

The statutes of the LORD are right, rejoicing the heart; The commandment of the LORD is pure, enlightening the eyes; The fear of the LORD is clean, enduring forever; The judgments of the LORD are true and righteous altogether. More to be desired are they than gold, Yea, than much fine gold; Sweeter also than honey and the honeycomb.

- Psalm 19:8-10

22 *let not your heart be troubled*

- Set my mind on Christ
- Give Jesus my burdens
- Meditate on Scripture

- Read His Word
- Align my thoughts
- Talk with Jesus all day!

- Give His love to others
- Express Gratitude
- Rejoice in this day

MORNING PRAYER

Casting all your care upon Him, for He cares for you.
1Peter 5:7

EVENING PRAISE

Praise the LORD! Oh, give thanks to the LORD,
for He is good! For His mercy endures forever.
Psalm 106:1

SCRIPTURE FOR TODAY

GRATITUDE JOURNAL

1.

2.

TODAY'S AFFIRMATION

1. I love the entirety of the Word of God.

2.

3.

Let not your heart be troubled; you believe in God, believe also in Me. - John 14:1

Open my eyes, that I may see Wondrous things from Your law. - Psalm 119:18

1 Word

2 Observing

3 Reflecting

4 Doing

Praying

Our Father in heaven,
Hallowed be Your name.
Your kingdom come.
Your will be done
on earth as it is in heaven.
Give us this day our daily bread.
And forgive us our debts,
As we forgive our debtors.
And do not lead us into temptation,
But deliver us from the evil one.
For Yours is the kingdom and
the power and the glory forever.
Amen.

MATTHEW 6:9-13

praise & HONOR YOUR HEAVENLY FATHER

surrender YOUR WILL FOR HIS

ask FOR YOUR DAILY NEEDS & THE NEEDS OF OTHERS.

confess YOUR SINS & RECEIVE FORGIVENESS

forgive THOSE WHO HAVE HURT YOU

guidance ASK FOR PROTECTION & GUIDANCE AWAY FROM TEMPTATIONS

deliverance ASK FOR DELIVERANCE FROM THE SCHEMES OF THE EVIL ONE

worship GOD AND BE GRATEFUL FOR ALL HIS ATTRIBUTES

Bible Time
journal

YOUR *word* IS VERY *pure*

THEREFORE YOUR SERVANT — *loves it.*

PSALM 119:140

"
Your words were found,

and I ate them,

And Your word was

to me the joy and

rejoicing of my heart;

For I am called

by Your name,

O LORD God of hosts.

– Jeremiah 15:16

23 *let not your heart be troubled*

- Set my mind on Christ
- Give Jesus my burdens
- Meditate on Scripture

- Read His Word
- Align my thoughts
- Talk with Jesus all day!

- Give His love to others
- Express Gratitude
- Rejoice in this day

MORNING PRAYER

Casting all your care upon Him, for He cares for you.
1Peter 5:7

EVENING PRAISE

Praise the LORD! Oh, give thanks to the LORD,
for He is good! For His mercy endures forever.
Psalm 106:1

SCRIPTURE FOR TODAY

GRATITUDE JOURNAL

1.

2.

TODAY'S AFFIRMATION

1. I am called.

2.

3.

Let not your heart be troubled; you believe in God, believe also in Me. - John 14:1

Open my eyes, that I may see Wondrous things from Your law. - Psalm 119:18

1 Word

2 Observing

3 Reflecting

4 Doing

Praying

Our Father in heaven,
Hallowed be Your name.
Your kingdom come.
Your will be done
On earth as it is in heaven.
Give us this day our daily bread.
And forgive us our debts,
As we forgive our debtors.
And do not lead us into temptation,
But deliver us from the evil one.
For Yours is the kingdom and
the power and the glory forever.
Amen.

MATTHEW 6:9-13

praise & honor your
HEAVENLY FATHER

Surrender your will for His

ask for your daily needs & the
NEEDS OF OTHERS.

confess your sins & receive
FORGIVENESS

forgive those who have
HURT YOU

guidance ASK FOR PROTECTION
& GUIDANCE AWAY
FROM TEMPTATIONS

deliverance ASK FOR DELIVERANCE
FROM THE SCHEMES
OF THE EVIL ONE

worship GOD AND BE GRATEFUL
FOR ALL HIS ATTRIBUTES

Bible Time
journal

I, THEREFORE, THE PRISONER OF THE LORD, BESEECH YOU TO

walk worthy OF THE CALLING

WITH WHICH YOU WERE *called*

- EPHESIANS 4:1

"

AND DO NOT BE

conformed TO THIS WORLD,

BUT BE *transformed*

BY THE
renewing OF YOUR *mind*,

THAT YOU MAY PROVE WHAT IS THAT

good AND *acceptable* AND *perfect*

WILL OF GOD.

ROMANS 12:2

24 *let not your heart be troubled*

- ⬢ Set my mind on Christ
- ⬢ Give Jesus my burdens
- ⬢ Meditate on Scripture
- ⬢ Read His Word
- ⬢ Align my thoughts
- ⬢ Talk with Jesus all day!
- ⬢ Give His love to others
- ⬢ Express Gratitude
- ⬢ Rejoice in this day

MORNING PRAYER

Casting all your care upon Him, for He cares for you.
1Peter 5:7

EVENING PRAISE

Praise the LORD! Oh, give thanks to the LORD,
for He is good! For His mercy endures forever.
Psalm 106:1

SCRIPTURE FOR TODAY

GRATITUDE JOURNAL

1.

2.

TODAY'S AFFIRMATION

1. I am renewing my mind.

2.

3.

Let not your heart be troubled; you believe in God, believe also in Me. - John 14:1

Open my eyes, that I may see Wondrous things from Your law. - Psalm 119:18

1 Word

2 Observing

3 Reflecting

4 Doing

Praying

Our *Father* in heaven,
Hallowed be Your *name*.
Your *kingdom* come.
Your will be done
On earth as it is in *heaven*.
Give us this day our *daily* bread.
And *forgive* us our debts,
As we *forgive* our debtors.
And do not *lead* us into *temptation*,
But *deliver* us from the *evil* one.
For *Yours* is the *kingdom* and
the *power* and the *glory* forever.
Amen.

MATTHEW 6:9-13

praise & Honor Your
Heavenly Father

Surrender Your Will For His

ask For Your Daily Needs & The
Needs Of Others.

confess Your Sins & Receive
Forgiveness

forgive Those Who Have
Hurt You

guidance Ask For Protection
& Guidance Away
From Temptations

deliverance Ask For Deliverance
From The Schemes
Of The Evil One

worship God And Be Grateful
For All His Attributes

Bible Time
journal

IN EVERYTHING *give thanks* FOR THIS IS
THE WILL OF GOD IN *Christ Jesus*
for you.
— 1Thessalonians 5:18

"

Let all bitterness, wrath, anger, clamor, and evil speaking be put away from you, with all malice. And be kind to one another, tenderhearted, forgiving one another, even as God in Christ forgave you

- Ephesians 4:31-32

25 let not your heart be troubled

Date:
S / M / T / W / T / F / S

- ⬡ Set my mind on Christ
- ⬡ Give Jesus my burdens
- ⬡ Meditate on Scripture
- ⬡ Read His Word
- ⬡ Align my thoughts
- ⬡ Talk with Jesus all day!
- ⬡ Give His love to others
- ⬡ Express Gratitude
- ⬡ Rejoice in this day

MORNING PRAYER

Casting all your care upon Him, for He cares for you.
1Peter 5:7

EVENING PRAISE

Praise the LORD! Oh, give thanks to the LORD,
for He is good! For His mercy endures forever.
Psalm 106:1

SCRIPTURE FOR TODAY

GRATITUDE JOURNAL

1.

2.

TODAY'S AFFIRMATION

1. I am kind, tenderhearted & forgiving.

2.

3.

Let not your heart be troubled; you believe in God, believe also in Me. - John 14:1

Open my eyes, that I may see Wondrous things from Your law. - Psalm 119:18

1 Word

2 Observing

3 Reflecting

4 Doing

Praying

Our Father in heaven,
Hallowed be Your name.
Your kingdom come.
Your will be done
on earth as it is in heaven.
Give us this day our daily bread.
And forgive us our debts,
as we forgive our debtors.
And do not lead us into temptation,
But deliver us from the evil one.
For Yours is the kingdom and
the power and the glory forever.
Amen.

MATTHEW 6:9-13

praise & HONOR YOUR
HEAVENLY FATHER

surrender YOUR WILL FOR HIS

ask FOR YOUR DAILY NEEDS & THE
NEEDS OF OTHERS.

confess YOUR SINS & RECEIVE
FORGIVENESS

forgive THOSE WHO HAVE
HURT YOU

guidance ASK FOR PROTECTION
& GUIDANCE AWAY
FROM TEMPTATIONS

deliverance ASK FOR DELIVERANCE
FROM THE SCHEMES
OF THE EVIL ONE

worship GOD AND BE GRATEFUL
FOR ALL HIS ATTRIBUTES

Bible Time
journal

LET NO *corrupt word* PROCEED FROM YOUR MOUTH, BUT WHAT IS GOOD FOR NECESSARY *edification*, THAT IT MAY IMPART *grace* TO THE HEARERS.

– EPHESIANS 4:29

"

Therefore be imitators of God as dear children. And walk in love, as Christ also has loved us and given Himself for us, an offering and a sacrifice to God for a sweet-smelling aroma.

- Ephesians 5:1-2

26 let not your heart be troubled

Date:
S / M / T / W / T / F / S

⬡ Set my mind on Christ
⬡ Give Jesus my burdens
⬡ Meditate on Scripture

⬡ Read His Word
⬡ Align my thoughts
⬡ Talk with Jesus all day!

⬡ Give His love to others
⬡ Express Gratitude
⬡ Rejoice in this day

MORNING PRAYER

Casting all your care upon Him, for He cares for you.
1Peter 5:7

EVENING PRAISE

Praise the LORD! Oh, give thanks to the LORD,
for He is good! For His mercy endures forever.
Psalm 106:1

SCRIPTURE FOR TODAY

GRATITUDE JOURNAL

1.

2.

TODAY'S AFFIRMATION

1. I imitate God. I walk in love.

2.

3.

Let not your heart be troubled; you believe in God, believe also in Me. - John 14:1

Open my eyes, that I may see Wondrous things from Your law. - Psalm 119:18

1 Word

2 Observing

3 Reflecting

4 Doing

Praying

Our Father in heaven,
Hallowed be Your name.
Your kingdom come.
Your will be done
On earth as it is in heaven.
Give us this day our daily bread.
And forgive us our debts,
As we forgive our debtors.
And do not lead us into temptation,
But deliver us from the evil one.
For Yours is the kingdom and
The power and the glory forever.
Amen.

MATTHEW 6:9-13

praise & HONOR YOUR
HEAVENLY FATHER

Surrender YOUR WILL FOR HIS

ask FOR YOUR DAILY NEEDS & THE
NEEDS OF OTHERS.

confess YOUR SINS & RECEIVE
FORGIVENESS

forgive THOSE WHO HAVE
HURT YOU

guidance ASK FOR PROTECTION
& GUIDANCE AWAY
FROM TEMPTATIONS

deliverance ASK FOR DELIVERANCE
FROM THE SCHEMES
OF THE EVIL ONE

worship GOD AND BE GRATEFUL
FOR ALL HIS ATTRIBUTES

Bible Time
journal

THIS IS *love'* THAT WE *walk according* TO HIS COMMANDMENTS...

– 2JOHN 1:6

"

But the fruit of the Spirit is love, joy, peace, longsuffering, kindness, goodness, faithfulness, gentleness, self-control. Against such there is no law.

-Galatians 5:22-23

27 let not your heart be troubled

Date:
S / M / T / W / T / F / S

- ⬡ Set my mind on Christ
- ⬡ Give Jesus my burdens
- ⬡ Meditate on Scripture
- ⬡ Read His Word
- ⬡ Align my thoughts
- ⬡ Talk with Jesus all day!
- ⬡ Give His love to others
- ⬡ Express Gratitude
- ⬡ Rejoice in this day

MORNING PRAYER

Casting all your care upon Him, for He cares for you.
1Peter 5:7

EVENING PRAISE

Praise the LORD! Oh, give thanks to the LORD,
for He is good! For His mercy endures forever.
Psalm 106:1

SCRIPTURE FOR TODAY

GRATITUDE JOURNAL

1.

2.

TODAY'S AFFIRMATION

1. *I have the fruit of the Spirit.*

2.

3.

Let not your heart be troubled; you believe in God, believe also in Me. - John 14:1

Open my eyes, that I may see Wondrous things from Your law. - Psalm 119:18

1 Word

2 Observing

3 Reflecting

4 Doing

Praying

Our Father in heaven,
Hallowed be Your name.
Your kingdom come.
Your will be done
on earth as it is in heaven.
Give us this day our daily bread.
And forgive us our debts,
as we forgive our debtors.
And do not lead us into temptation,
But deliver us from the evil one.
For Yours is the kingdom and
the power and the glory forever.
Amen.

MATTHEW 6:9-13

praise & honor your
heavenly father

surrender your will for His

ask for your daily needs & the
needs of others.

confess your sins & receive
forgiveness

forgive those who have
hurt you

guidance ask for protection
& guidance away
from temptations

deliverance ask for deliverance
from the schemes
of the evil one

worship god and be grateful
for all his attributes

Bible Time
journal

AND NOW ABIDE *faith, hope, love,* THESE THREE:

BUT THE GREATEST OF THESE IS *love.* 1CORINTHIANS 13:13

"

Be kindly affectionate to

one another with brotherly love,

in honor giving preference to

one another: not lagging in diligence,

fervent in spirit, serving the Lord;

rejoicing in hope, patient in tribulation,

continuing steadfastly in prayer;

distributing to the needs of the saints,

given to hospitality.

- Romans 12:10-13

28 *let not your heart be troubled*

- ⬡ Set my mind on Christ
- ⬡ Give Jesus my burdens
- ⬡ Meditate on Scripture
- ⬡ Read His Word
- ⬡ Align my thoughts
- ⬡ Talk with Jesus all day!
- ⬡ Give His love to others
- ⬡ Express Gratitude
- ⬡ Rejoice in this day

MORNING PRAYER

*Casting all your care upon Him, for He cares for you.
1Peter 5:7*

EVENING PRAISE

*Praise the LORD! Oh, give thanks to the LORD,
for He is good! For His mercy endures forever.
Psalm 106:1*

SCRIPTURE FOR TODAY

GRATITUDE JOURNAL

1.

2.

TODAY'S AFFIRMATION

1. *I give preference to others.*

3.

2.

Let not your heart be troubled; you believe in God, believe also in Me. - John 14:1

Open my eyes, that I may see Wondrous things from Your law. - Psalm 119:18

1 Word

2 Observing

3 Reflecting

4 Doing

Praying

Our Father in heaven,
Hallowed be Your name.
Your kingdom come.
Your will be done
on earth as it is in heaven.
Give us this day our daily bread.
And forgive us our debts,
as we forgive our debtors.
And do not lead us into temptation,
But deliver us from the evil one.
For Yours is the kingdom and
the power and the glory forever.
Amen.

MATTHEW 6:9-13

praise & HONOR YOUR
HEAVENLY FATHER

Surrender YOUR WILL FOR HIS

ask FOR YOUR DAILY NEEDS & THE
NEEDS OF OTHERS.

confess YOUR SINS & RECEIVE
FORGIVENESS

forgive THOSE WHO HAVE
HURT YOU

guidance ASK FOR PROTECTION
& GUIDANCE AWAY
FROM TEMPTATIONS

deliverance ASK FOR DELIVERANCE
FROM THE SCHEMES
OF THE EVIL ONE

worship GOD AND BE GRATEFUL
FOR ALL HIS ATTRIBUTES

Bible Time journal

SINCE YOU HAVE PURIFIED YOUR SOULS IN OBEYING THE TRUTH THROUGH THE SPIRIT

sincere love of the brethren, love one another

fervently WITH A PURE *heart.*

- 1Peter 1:22

"

Then I looked, and I heard the voice of many angels around the throne, the living creatures, and the elders; and the number of them was ten thousand times ten thousand, and thousands of thousands, saying with a loud voice:

"*Worthy* is the Lamb who was slain To receive power and riches and wisdom, And strength and honor and glory and blessing!"

And every creature which is in heaven and on the earth and under the earth and such as are in the sea, and all that are in them,
I heard saying:

"*Blessing* and honor and glory and power be to Him who sits on the throne, And to the Lamb, forever and ever!"

- Revelation 5:11-13

29 *let not your heart be troubled*

⬡ Set my mind on Christ   ⬡ Read His Word   ⬡ Give His love to others

⬡ Give Jesus my burdens   ⬡ Align my thoughts   ⬡ Express Gratitude

⬡ Meditate on Scripture   ⬡ Talk with Jesus all day!   ⬡ Rejoice in this day

MORNING PRAYER

Casting all your care upon Him, for He cares for you.
1Peter 5:7

EVENING PRAISE

Praise the LORD! Oh, give thanks to the LORD,
for He is good! For His mercy endures forever.
Psalm 106:1

SCRIPTURE FOR TODAY

GRATITUDE JOURNAL

1.

2.

TODAY'S AFFIRMATION

1. *Jesus is worthy of all my praise.*

2.

3.

Let not your heart be troubled; you believe in God, believe also in Me. - John 14:1

Open my eyes, that I may see Wondrous things from Your law. - Psalm 119:18

1 Word

2 Observing

3 Reflecting

4 Doing

Praying

Our Father in heaven,
Hallowed be Your name.
Your kingdom come.
Your will be done
On earth as it is in heaven.
Give us this day our daily bread.
And forgive us our debts,
As we forgive our debtors.
And do not lead us into temptation,
But deliver us from the evil one.
For Yours is the kingdom and
The power and the glory forever.
Amen.

MATTHEW 6:9-13

praise & HONOR YOUR HEAVENLY FATHER

surrender YOUR WILL FOR HIS

ask FOR YOUR DAILY NEEDS & THE NEEDS OF OTHERS.

confess YOUR SINS & RECEIVE FORGIVENESS

forgive THOSE WHO HAVE HURT YOU

guidance ASK FOR PROTECTION & GUIDANCE AWAY FROM TEMPTATIONS

deliverance ASK FOR DELIVERANCE FROM THE SCHEMES OF THE EVIL ONE

worship GOD AND BE GRATEFUL FOR ALL HIS ATTRIBUTES

Bible Time
journal

I WILL *call upon* THE LORD WHO IS *worthy* TO BE *praised* . . .

- PSALM 18:3

"

I have fought the good fight.

I have finished the race.

I have kept the faith

Finally, there is laid up for me the

crown of righteousness, which

THE LORD the righteous Judge,

will give to me on that Day,

and not to me only but also

to all who have loved His appearing

- 2Timothy 4: 7-8

30 *let not your heart be troubled*

- ⬡ Set my mind on Christ
- ⬡ Give Jesus my burdens
- ⬡ Meditate on Scripture
- ⬡ Read His Word
- ⬡ Align my thoughts
- ⬡ Talk with Jesus all day!
- ⬡ Give His love to others
- ⬡ Express Gratitude
- ⬡ Rejoice in this day

MORNING PRAYER

Casting all your care upon Him, for He cares for you.
1Peter 5:7

EVENING PRAISE

Praise the LORD! Oh, give thanks to the LORD,
for He is good! For His mercy endures forever.
Psalm 106:1

SCRIPTURE FOR TODAY

GRATITUDE JOURNAL

1.

2.

TODAY'S AFFIRMATION

1. *I run my race with endurance.*

2.

3.

Let not your heart be troubled; you believe in God, believe also in Me. - John 14:1

Open my eyes, that I may see Wondrous things from Your law. - Psalm 119:18

1 Word

2 Observing

3 Reflecting

4 Doing

Praying

Our Father in heaven,
Hallowed be Your name.
Your kingdom come.
Your will be done
On earth as it is in heaven.
Give us this day our daily bread.
And forgive us our debts,
As we forgive our debtors.
And do not lead us into temptation,
But deliver us from the evil one.
For Yours is the kingdom and
the power and the glory forever.
Amen.

MATTHEW 6:9-13

praise & HONOR YOUR
HEAVENLY FATHER

surrender YOUR WILL FOR HIS

ask FOR YOUR DAILY NEEDS & THE
NEEDS OF OTHERS.

confess YOUR SINS & RECEIVE
FORGIVENESS

forgive THOSE WHO HAVE
HURT YOU

guidance ASK FOR PROTECTION
& GUIDANCE AWAY
FROM TEMPTATIONS

deliverance ASK FOR DELIVERANCE
FROM THE SCHEMES
OF THE EVIL ONE

worship GOD AND BE GRATEFUL
FOR ALL HIS ATTRIBUTES

Bible Time
journal

Therefore WE ALSO, SINCE WE ARE SURROUNDED BY SO GREAT A CLOUD OF WITNESSES, LET US LAY ASIDE EVERY WEIGHT, AND THE SIN WHICH SO EASILY ENSNARES US, AND LET US *run with endurance the race that is set before us.*

- HEBREWS 12:1

Your prayer requests

Write out your prayer requests. *"Ask, and it will be given to you; seek, and you will find; knock, and it will be opened to you."* - Matthew 7:7   Believe it!

date   requests

Your prayer answers

Write out how God answered your prayers. *"For everyone who asks receives, and he who seeks finds, and to him who knocks it will be opened. - Matthew 7:8*

date   answers

Bible Time
conclusion

Spend some time reflecting on each of your Bible Time experiences with the LORD. Did God open your eyes to behold wondrous things in His Word? Write out your reflections of your journey and how Jesus worked in your life. Write out a prayer of praise and thanksgiving.

THE *Abundant Life*

IS YOURS TO SEIZE!

Meet Janette

Janette Henning is coauthor of the life-changing books Melissa, If One Life . . . , and the Devotional Journal - Craving Intimacy with God, along with her daughter Melissa Camp. She is described by her readers as a powerful storyteller, a beautiful writer, inspiring, vulnerable, sharing the raw pieces of her heart with words that resonate deep in the soul.

Janette is passionate about sharing Melissa's life, her journals, and the power of one life surrendered to Christ. She is a fervent follower of Jesus Christ, a wife, a mother of four, and a grandmother of eight. She has been a pastor's wife, a church planter, a women's minister, a Bible Study writer, a Bible teacher, and a conference speaker, as well as a real estate agent teaming with her husband Mark, in San Diego County. They live in the beach community of Encinitas, California.

Melissa & Mom

Melissa Lynn Camp lived her life in a passionate pursuit of knowing God intimately - she craved it! Her journals reveal her great love for Jesus and she longed to share them with the world. Her desire was to impact young women to walk closely with God and she is fulfilling that desire everyday. Not just one, but millions have been inspired and impacted by her life and her words.

Melissa married Jeremy Camp on October 21, 2000; they lived close to the beach in Carlsbad, California, until her home going on February 5, 2001. Their love story was the inspiration for the film I Still Believe. You can read Melissa's journals and experience their beautiful love story in the book, Melissa If One Life . . . .. Visit her website, melissalynncamp.com for more information and inspiration.

Connect with me

I write to encourage you, as my daughter Melissa would, that this amazing, supernatural, powerful, and abundant life is yours to seize. You have gifts and abilities uniquely given to you to bring glory to God and to impact others for eternity. There is a spectacular plan and purpose for your life - even if your life is interrupted, unexpected, deeply wounded, scarred or disappointing to you. Don't be discouraged dear one. God is working in every detail to show off His splendor through your life. Seize the life that is "more" abundant than you could ever imagine! I'm here to encourage you on your journey. Connect with me anytime.

janette@ifonelife.com

@janettehenning   @melissaifonelife

let's get social!

janette_henning   melissa_if_one_life

Melissa Henning Camp

janettehenning

melissalynncamp.com   janettehenning.com   janettehenning.my.canva.site

I HAVE COME THAT THEY MAY HAVE *life*, AND THAT THEY MAY HAVE IT MORE *abundantly*.

JOHN 10:10

FREE *gifts* FOR YOU

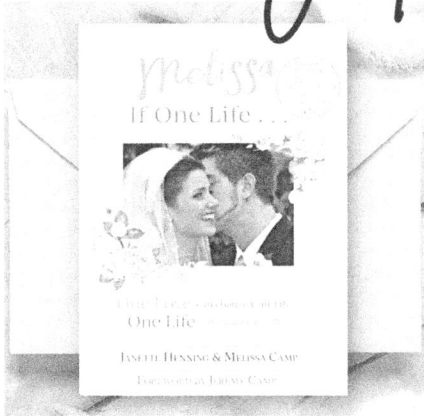

MELISSA'S STORY

Melissa, If One Life . . .
Inspiration for the film
I STILL BELIEVE

FREE CHAPTER

DEVO-JOURNAL

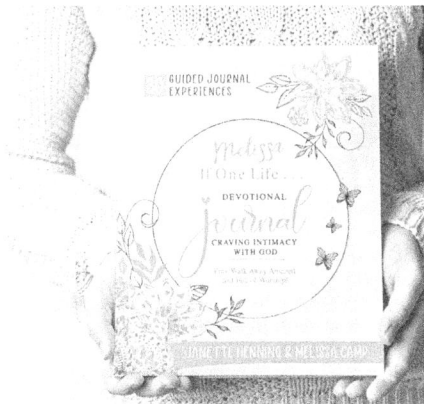

Melissa, If One Life . . .
Devotional Journal
Craving Intimacy with God

3 DAYS FREE

DEVOTIONAL PRAYER JOURNAL

30 Day Quiet Time
Devotional Prayer Journal
Be Jesus Strong!

3 DAYS FREE

LOVE, JOY & HOPE . . . THROUGH TRIALS

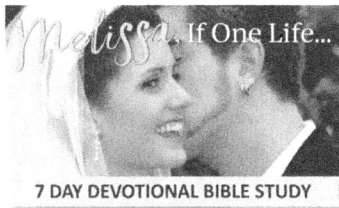

7 DAY DEVOTIONAL BIBLE STUDY

joy love hope

In Honor & Appreciation of

MELISSA LYNN CAMP

Journal Entry

" *I pray that my life will be a living sacrifice, holy and blameless to You Father. I pray that I will be upheld when I fall, and lifted up when I bow down. Father, humble me; break me, mold me into the woman you intend, and will me to be. I pray that my eyes will open to see the will of You. Lord. I pray my #1 desire always will be to seek Your face. Oh, how I love You Lord. I lift up the Holy, Righteous, Perfect Name, Jesus Christ.*

The Lord is faithful to complete all his promises. The Lord loves all those who love Him. The Lord upholds all those who fall down and the Lord lifts up all those who are bowed down.

And this is my prayer "that your love may abound still more and more in knowledge and all discernment, that you may approve the things that are excellent, that you may be sincere and without offense till the day of Christ, being filled with the fruits of righteousness which are by Jesus Christ, to the glory and praise of God." Philippians 1:9-11 **"**

Melissa

HE HAS MADE HIS WONDERFUL WORKS TO BE REMEMBERED;
THE LORD IS GRACIOUS AND FULL OF COMPASSION.
- PSALM 111:4

Made in the USA
Las Vegas, NV
10 March 2023